URBAN LEGEND

GORDON BOSTIC

PRIMIX
PUBLISHING
THE WRITE CHOICE

Primix Publishing
East Brunswick Office Evolution
1 Tower Center Boulevard, Ste 1510
East Brunswick, NJ 08816
www.primixpublishing.com
Phone: 1-800-538-5788

Published by Primix Publishing: 01/27/2025

ISBN: 979-8-88703-416-4(sc)
ISBN: 979-8-88703-417-1(c)

Library of Congress Control Number: 2024917435

CONTENTS

THE LEGEND

The legend called them demantoids
Who're neither man nor beast.
They preyed upon humanity
On whom they loved to feast.

The legends were, that long ago,
A lizard race survived.
That man had driven underground
Where it had grown and thrived.

It said they were intelligent.
Perhaps, more so than man.
Where man was now the primitive
Though not due to some plan.

It said they foraged late at night
And man had been their prey.
So, anyone alone at night
May find a price they'd pay.

Though few gave the legend credence
The stories did persist.
Where infrequently a murder
Seemed to prove they exist.

THE STATE OF THE CITY

The city once was beautiful
But succumbed to hard times.
For what the Mayor did to it
She should be charged with crimes.

Their neighborhoods had grown unsafe
With drug use on the rise.
And thus, civility had waned
In courtesy's demise.

Now gangs had formed that ruled the streets
With pure impunity.
Because police found hands were tied
Due to their scrutiny.

The welfare state had grown so large
There was no need of pride.
For all of those who'd foot the bill
Found success was denied.

The crime rate suddenly had spiked
And taxes were too high.
A recent exodus occurred
But Mayor knew not why.

THE MAYOR

The Mayor ruled as she saw fit
Regardless of the law.
For she had no opposition
To the vision she saw.

The Mayor illegitimate
In things that she would do.
Because the payout she believed
Was what she had been due.

The Mayor was unscrupulous
Because she had no fear.
For there was no opposition
To the job she held dear.

Her power was unlimited
Because there were no checks.
The City Council was a joke
As all were total wrecks.

THE PARK

A large expanse of real estate
The city set aside.
That had become its greatest joy
Which it had viewed with pride.

At first, it had been well maintained
As funds were set aside.
With grasses neatly manicured
And lots of care supplied.

But over time the park declined
From government neglect.
Where money had been syphoned off
Brought undesired effect.

Now it became the focal point
Of parties late at night.
Although it was prohibited
Enforcement had been light.

So, there was still an element
That roamed the park at night.
Which clearly was unsavory
And casted a nasty light.

THE HOMELESS

The homeless population swelled
Under the Mayor's reign.
Though she would not acknowledge it
Nor thought would entertain.

With mental institutions closed
Some had no place to go.
And jobless rates at all-time highs
Some faced an all-time low.

The streets were overrun with them
And shelters had been full.
Their advocates had done their best
But truly had no pull.

The Mayor addressed the problem
With a new tax increase.
Which meant that more jobs had been lost
As action was caprice.

She said these funds were set aside
To help those most in need.
But funds had seemed to disappear
Through carelessness or greed.

MURPHY

He was the Mayor's lieutenant
And Murphy was his name.
As the perfect politician
He'd proved to have no shame.

While Murphy ran the day to day
The Mayor's focus laid
In dealing with the media
Where politics were played.

There were few who'd trusted Murphy
As he'd a slimy feel.
For each assurance that he gave
Most doubted had been real.

He reeked of insincerity
And had a phony smile.
He claimed he was a friend to all
Much like a crocodile.

The Mayor had been sleazy, too,
But sometimes seemed sincere.
While Murphy a conniving whore
That few would dare go near.

GAIL KENT

Gail Kent gained notoriety
For stances that she took.
She was a homeless advocate
Who'd not followed the book.

She had not feared the government,
In fact, she showed contempt.
It had responsibilities
Though tried to be exempt.

She had organized some rallies
That marched on City Hall
With attempts to shame the Mayor
Who'd done nothing at all.

She was no friend of the Mayor
As she found her a pain.
Where if she could find a reason
The woman she'd detain.

But what most people had not known
Was her past history.
They only saw the advocate
Not how she came to be.

Her faith had made her who she was
With hope who she'd become.
For it was her goal and mission
Her past to overcome.

For she had once been homeless, too,
Where reason she'd survive
Was she surrendered unto God
Whose grace kept her alive.

She'd known the hardships that they knew,
The depression and fear.
It was her faith that carried her
And what had brought her here.

Her faith was what supported her
Through hard times she had known.
And now, her faith was telling her
Compassion must be shown.

MURPHY'S ASSOCIATES

Murphy had some associates
That seemed unsavory.
It's rare that any said a word
Though looks had been wary.

They all possessed a certain air
That trouble was their way.
Where most were intimidated
And tried to stay away.

They'd shown a sense of loyalty
That went beyond bizarre.
As though whatever Murphy asked
They'd not believed too far.

None knew what purpose they had served.
Few even knew a name.
But they'd always be with Murphy
As Murphy they would frame.

Some thought they were security
But that could not be true.
For that had not been budgeted
So, no one had a clue.

THE BEAR

The bear it seemed slipped into town
In search of a free meal.
Whatever intercepted it
Gave them an eerie feel.

The bear had weighed eight hundred pounds
And stood nearly eight feet.
Whatever had torn into it
Was truly not discrete.

For the bear was torn asunder
With its carcass a shell.
It seemed whatever killed the bear
Had truly eaten well.

The coroner had been disturbed
To think he'd seen it all.
For this had been a travesty
That made his stomach crawl.

While police had found no reason
To signal an alarm.
They were concerned this animal
Could really cause some harm.

Though it was not unusual
To find a bear in town.
The oddity not knowing what
Had taken the bear down.

There'd been reports that fam'ly pets
Began to disappear.
They found it no emergency
Though thought it kind of queer.

The media had covered it
But had shown no concern.
They aired it as a filler piece
As they had time to burn.

It had not been an oddity
Bears wandered into town.
But what had been unusual
Was what took the bear down.

BEHIND THE SCENES

Behind the scenes there was concern
About what had occurred.
They had no clue what killed the bear
As no signs were procured.

There'd been no clear-cut evidence
So, no report prepared.
The Mayor was incredulous
How much police had cared.

She'd thought that they'd gone overboard
In trying to explain
What had been an act of nature.
Which she had thought was plain.

The Chief had said that his concern
Was how something that huge
Could simply be just ripped apart
As from a centrifuge.

It was clear there was a danger
That lurked somewhere in town.
But they possessed no single clue
To what brought the bear down.

The Chief had said they needed help
And wished to bring some in.
Perhaps from the Academy
To give a diff'rent spin.

JUST AN ACT OF NATURE

When the Mayor had been questioned
Her thoughts about the bear.
At first, she had dismissed the fact
That anyone should care.

It was just an act of nature
And simply nothing more.
Although it was a rarity
It had happened before.

Then they asked about what killed it.
Reports were it's immense.
The Mayor claimed ongoing case
With no facts to dispense.

The Mayor had grown bored with it
That danger was perceived.
It only was a big brown bear
Some other beast had cleaved.

MATT DANIELS

Matt Daniels was the detective
That was assigned the case.
Who felt no sense of urgency
As he'd no clues to chase.

Though he found that he was puzzled.
Why should they even care?
For there'd been no person murdered.
It simply was a bear.

Yet, when given his assignment
No questions did he ask.
He thought there must be a reason
He'd been given this task.

Although he found he must admit
He'd not known where to start.
For there had been no evidence
And he was not that smart.

THE FALSE ADVOCATE

The Mayor was a hypocrite
Who to the people pledged
Their homeless would have her support
Though actions always hedged.

But once election had been won
She turned her back again.
Believing that they were a blight
Who earned the fix they're in.

She claimed to be their advocate
Until it was assured
Her re-election was confirmed
Then promises obscured.

For it was the same old story
That's told ev'ry four years.
The promises are quick to come
But none ever appears.

Where all of her assurances
Had by the wayside laid.
Where there was nothing left to them
But knowing they were played.

GAIL'S PLEAS

The Mayor saw that she was back
And would not go away.
Her re-election was assured
But Gail was here to stay.

Gail pleaded with authorities
To help them in their need.
But deaf ears had been turned to her
As they'd covet their greed.

For those who held authority
Were heartless and unkind.
Who thought the homeless unworthy
So, to them had been blind.

Their suits had been extravagant
Where no expense was spared.
And, though, the homeless were their charge
It seemed they had not cared.

Their offices were more than swank.
Remodeled at great cost.
Though what the homeless had been due
They claimed had all been lost.

Gail demanded she make changes
To deal with this affair
Or the Mayor would feel pressure
Beyond Gail's normal flair.

THE THUNDERBIRDS

The Thunderbirds had been a gang
To which Matt once belonged.
Where now he was a legacy
Which Matt had found two pronged.

Though once he had been one of them
He'd now become a cop.
And, though, they still befriended him
Their caution would not stop.

It's their belief they owned the park
As each night after dark
They gather with their wine and beer,
And girls with whom to spark.

Matt went to them to see if they
Knew something of the bear
For he knew they were far reaching
And had eyes ev'rywhere.

But they claimed they had no knowledge
And never saw the bear.
Nor anything unusual
Of which they were aware.

Matt left them to their childish ways
He felt that he'd outgrown.
But found it truly circumspect
That nothing had they known.

He knew if they had seen the bear
A challenge would be made.
And knowing them, it's possible,
Too drunk to be afraid.

But it's the bear that had been maimed
So, clearly, it's not them.
Thus, once again he faced square one
With no clues left to him.

TWO DIFFERENT WORLDS

As Gail stormed out of City Hall
She had bumped into Matt.
Gail knew that he was sweet on her
So, she had stopped to chat.

Though they were from two diff'rent worlds
Gail sensed in Matt some charm.
She knew he was a decent man
Who had meant her no harm.

She asked why he's at City Hall.
Matt said he had a case.
Where within the Hall of Records,
Something he had to trace.

Then Matt asked her out to dinner.
Gail felt she must decline.
She'd no wish to get serious
Though friendship would be fine.

They both then parted on good terms,
Each going their own way.
Gail had thought it's nice to see him.
Matt thought she got away.

SARGE

The one called Sarge had been a friend
Gail spoke to ev'ryday.
He was a grizzled veteran
Who'd no place else to stay.

He was devoid of family
So, at his service end
The streets became what he called home
Where the weak he'd defend.

Though Sarge had been a lonely man,
He also was quite proud.
His visage was so serious
He stood out from the crowd.

He'd been to war at least three times
And tours he served were eight.
He had been wounded seven times
But six he claimed were fate.

He had not been the only one
Who'd taken to the street.
For many who had chose to serve
Found new lives hard to greet.

A CALL FOR AUDIT

The media picked up on it
And would not let it go.
The allegations that Gail made
It somehow came to know.

The Mayor's office was besieged
With confirmation sought
If what Gail claimed was really true
And Mayor had been caught.

The media then turned to Gail
As City Hall went mute.
They knew she'd gone to war with them
And strong was their dispute.

For the ones who ran the shelters
Were evil and corrupt.
What little peace the homeless found
They gladly would disrupt.

They lived on the amenities
The homeless had been due.
But claimed with what they're budgeted
There's little they could do.

In fact, there're none who'd intercede
In what the homeless faced.
They spent their time in pocketing
That which they'd not wished traced.

She said she'd asked the FBI
With audit her request.
The funds she thought the homeless due
She feared had been suppressed.

Her fear had been the ones in charge
Had syphoned funds away.
Where those who showed the greatest need
Would be the ones who'd pay.

UNDER FIRE

Her enemies had seen their chance
While she was under fire.
They saw the opportunity
To force her to retire.

The voters thought response was weak
Though none had truly cared.
The homeless they would sacrifice
If citizens were spared.

The Mayor, though, was under fire
As she misunderstood.
It's not as though the people cared
But wanted to look good.

The Mayor was the one in charge
Thus, she must bear the blame.
She claimed that efforts had been made
But results were the same.

The Mayor had come under fire
For she'd not done enough
To be rid of the corruption
That made their lives so tough.

The media had hounded her
And asked her to explain
Why were the homeless sacrificed
While office she'd retain.

Her poll numbers began to slip
With what the fire had cost.
While the favor of the public
It seemed that she had lost.

BEGINNING OF THE AUDIT

Pat Phillips of the FBI
Had found it very clear
The Mayor had embezzled funds
As books she'd engineer.

The money she would allocate
Had brought her dividends
Where ev'ry dollar that she spent
A portion went to friends.

Pat liked how nicely it was done.
All wrapped up in a bow.
As though someone uncovered it
And left it there for show.

It's clear that someone set her up
But evidence was plain.
The Mayor had embezzled funds
And for her private gain.

Pat said the further that he dug
The more he'd come to know.
For now, it's clear the Mayor's done
And would be first to go.

The evidence that she denied
Had all been proven true.
The Mayor knew she was betrayed
But not whom vengeance due.

THE MAYOR'S DEMISE

The secrets that she coveted
And tried hard to conceal.
Her enemies had known them all
And chosen to reveal.

The Mayor's days were numbered now
With writing on the wall.
She locked herself inside her room
With choice to end it all.

While Murphy was the next in line
Ascending to the role
To claim the power that he craved
And thus, to seize control.

But when the Mayor was exposed
She saw one option out.
She'd not face humiliation
Which this had been about.

The Mayor then had known defeat
And knew her days were done.
She locked herself inside her room
Where she could use her gun.

MURPHY'S LAMENT

Murphy claimed he was horrified
In how this all should end.
The Mayor was his champion
And, also, was a friend.

He hated that it came to this
But he was unaware
The Mayor an impediment
Who'd long since ceased to care.

Though Murphy said in his lament
He's sad to see her go.
But confident his policies
Would help the city grow.

Divisions were what he'd address
As there were more than few.
His goal was to bring unity
Which he thought long past due.

The homeless, too, he'd focus on
And recognize their plight.
He, too, would be an advocate
And try to do them right.

Though Gail agreed appear with him
As his announcement made.
She found she'd trusted not a word
But saw the game he played.

For there was never a lament
To find the Mayor dead.
For Murphy, just a stepping stone
To where he would be led.

MICHELLE'S DISAPPEARANCE

When the reports had first come in
Police showed no concern.
Although it was unusual
They thought she would return.

For ev'ry now and then, it seemed,
Michelle would run away.
Where she'd be gone a couple days
Then return home to stay.

But this time had been different
As she'd been gone four days.
She'd not before been gone that long
Where family was crazed.

Police had checked her common haunts
But no one there had said
Michelle had been there recently
Which had led some to dread.

It purely was by accident
Her body had been found.
A jogger stumbled over it,
As it littered the ground.

It was a gruesome spectacle
That the police had found.
Her body had been ripped apart
With pieces spread around.

This was much more than a murder.
It seemed more like a feast.
As though Michelle wandered into
The lair of some beast.

When Matt arrived upon the scene
It caught him by surprise.
He gagged and choked despite the fact
He'd not believed his eyes.

Although he'd never been to war
Some ugly sights he'd seen.
But this by far had been the worse
Of any true crime scene.

Matt told some officers to search
For any who'd witness.
Though it seemed highly unlikely
To this one would confess.

Her parents overcome with grief
To hear that she was dead.
But Matt refused to say it looked
Like something on her fed.

THE SUSPECTS

There was a gang that roamed the park.
A fact that was well-known.
Police had tried to chase them out
But park they seemed to own.

They rounded up the worthless scum
And questioned them till light.
But none of them had dared confess
They'd seen Michelle that night.

They could find no other suspects
Until they noticed Sarge.
For he would wander through the park
And he was very large.

Police had dared to question him
And showed him no respect.
For it had been made clear to him
He was their prime suspect.

When Gail had heard Sarge was picked up
And held for questioning.
All saw Gail was beside herself
And war ready to bring.

She stormed into the station house
Demanding his release.
They had no right in holding him
Beyond being caprice.

Reluctantly, police complied
For lack of evidence.
Although Sarge had no alibi
To offer in defense.

THE TRANSITION

Although Murphy now was Mayor
There's little that had changed.
He pursued the same policies
The dead Mayor arranged.

The law suit was of no concern
For if the suit was lost
The taxpayers would cover it
As they would bear the cost.

The audit, too, he had ignored
Believing it no threat.
The perpetrator had been caught
And punishment was met.

Though the homeless he abandoned
Despite what he had swore.
For, now, his status was secure,
He needed them no more.

So now Murphy as the Mayor
Had one thing left to do.
Which was to fool constituents
His promises came true.

MEDIA REPORTS

The news had been consumed with it
As on it they had dwelled.
Where they would wildly speculate
As details were withheld.

But the media spoke of it
As if it had been there.
The question Matt would have to ask.
How was it so aware?

Matt felt it was indelicate
With details it'd report.
Matt thought about the family
Whose shock he tried to thwart.

Though it's clear the depth of detail
The media was fed
Had proven that there was a leak
Through which facts had been bled.

Although as far as Matt had known,
No details were released.
So, another problem surfaced
As his worries increased.

THE LAW SUIT

Michelle's family had been crushed
When they had heard the news.
For Matt was not up front with them
Where lawyers now were used.

As the city faced a law suit
That safety was ignored.
For years the park was dangerous
Yet, changes unexplored.

Their daughter had been brutalized
And someone had to pay.
Although she was a party girl
She'd need not die that way.

The law suit was an annoyance
With which Murphy must deal.
He had a feeling it would come
Which now was proven real.

While Murphy cursed the officer
That he had held to blame.
It seemed the facts that he relayed
Sparked them to file a claim.

Whatever cost this may incur
Murphy would willing pay.
As long as in the settlement
This all would go away.

The city offered settlement
In hope there'd be no trial.
Although responsibility
Were forced into denial.

GRASPING AT STRAWS

Matt thought police may have a point
As Gail's group had lived near
To where the body had been found
To, maybe, see or hear

If something seemed unusual
That they'd noticed that night.
Perhaps they'd even seen someone
That may not have seemed right.

Police had never questioned them
Believing waste of time.
As at least half were not lucid
And how they lived a crime.

But the homeless were observant
As they found need to be.
And they looked out for each other
So, ev'rything they'd see.

But whether they would talk or not
Had left him most concerned.
It was rare they'd speak to strangers
That he'd already learned.

Though he knew it was a long shot
As no clues meant no cause.
And in the end may only find
He'd been grasping at straws.

THE PRESS CONFERENCE

A panic had seemed imminent
With few details released.
The media had fanned the flames
As coverage increased.

Thus, Murphy went before the press
So, he could reassure
There was no reason for alarm
Of that, he had been sure.

The Mayor claimed the incident
Was no cause for concern.
For it was a lone occurrence
As far as they'd discern.

Investigations would proceed
Till answers had been found.
For now, people should be assured
That to the truth they're bound.

Then came the questions Murphy feared
To which he could not speak.
For certain things must stay secret
To find the one they'd seek.

Though media unsatisfied
With answers that he gave.
A girl was murdered on his watch
That loosely filled her grave.

UNTRUSTING OF POLICE

When Matt had first approached Gail's group
He sensed anger and fear.
They were not trusting of police
And that was very clear.

He tried approaching Gail herself
But he, she just ignored.
She was still angry about Sarge
And faith not yet restored.

Matt told her he was not at fault.
It had not been his call.
But a girl was murdered near there
As, maybe, she'd recall.

Then Gail had nodded her consent
And Matt approached the group.
He asked if they'd seen anything
But no one had a scoop.

Then Matt had thanked them for their time
And told them to be safe.
He said they should avoid the park
As it had seemed unsafe.

While Matt was just about to leave,
He turned to speak with Gail.
He asked again to have dinner.
Where Gail thought, "What the hell."

A NIGHT OUT

The place had seemed extravagant
Where Gail had been impressed.
Though not a place a cop would go.
At least, that's what Gail guessed.

The meal had been extremely good
And conversation light.
She'd no wish to admit to it
But was a pleasant night.

She was surprised she would enjoy
So much Matt's company.
He had a good sense of humor
Though a strange history.

Matt moved around from job to job
Till settled as a cop.
The paperwork was horrible
But action would not stop.

Matt wished to spend the night with her
But Gail had not agreed.
She had not known him well enough
That to that she'd concede.

Which proved to spoil the night for Gail
As she could not believe
That Matt had a preconception
To what he would receive.

THE SETTLEMENT

Their lawyers told them to prepare
As efforts would be made
To push the scandal to the side
And then they would be paid.

With money no impediment
As it had not been theirs.
The taxpayers would foot the bill
And be left unawares.

The tragedy it would concede
But wanted in return
Assurances this was the end
Even if more they'd learn.

The settlement was more than fair
Thought Michelle's family.
For the money had been more than they
Thought they would ever see.

AN AWKWARD SILENCE

When next Gail had run into Matt
An awkward silence fell.
Where both had felt embarrassment
And drew into a shell.

Though neither wished perceived as rude
They'd found little to say.
Instead, a strange uneasiness
Had forced them both to stay.

Gail said she'd liked the restaurant.
Matt said that he was glad.
But neither would elaborate
Nor nothing more to add.

At last, Gail had excused herself
As she was running late.
Matt said he had an interview
Where the guy may not wait.

The awkward silence made Gail feel
That she should be ashamed.
Perhaps, somehow, she'd led him on.
If so, she should be blamed.

MEGHAN

The sky had barely just gone dark
When Meghan looked around.
She'd been listening to music
But now worry she'd found.

The iPod she had come upon
Was lying in the street.
Where she hastily procured it
And made a quick retreat.

She'd heard the park had not been safe
After the sun went down.
Where she had lingered way too long
And may in panic drown.

She heard a rustle in the brush
And felt her breathing halt.
She had no clue which way to run
So, she'd avoid assault.

But in the dark, she had been blind
Where she'd stumbled and fell.
Her heart was racing recklessly
And terror could not quell.

The creature caught her by surprise
Where she'd no place to run.
She stared into its cold, dead eyes
And knew that she was done.

She prayed God would deliver her
But knew it's not to be.
The creature quickly took her down
As she screamed pleadingly.

Her fear so great, she felt no pain
As something in her plunged.
Preventing her from an escape
When then the creature lunged.

Her body had been ripped apart
When next day it was found.
And though the park had been in use,
Not one had heard a sound.

But officers had lost their lunch
When they came on the scene.
It was a gruesome spectacle
Like none they'd ever seen.

The body had been ripped apart
As though part of a feast.
Whatever was responsible
Was something less than beast.

THE NEW CORONER

Their coroner had broken down
After they found Michelle.
He could not lose the memory
And lived in his own hell.

So, the Mayor found a new one
Whose name was Amy Lynn.
She had bragged that nothing shocked her
Thus, she they had brought in.

Amy was a petite brunet
Who did not look the part.
Matt had been used to Doctor Reed
Who'd, seemingly, no heart.

Though she claimed nothing could shock her,
What she had seen that night
Had been nothing she'd imagined
So gruesome was the sight.

Matt rushed to her to offer aid
Believing she'd be sick.
He knew the feeling all too well
As it he tried to lick.

She thanked him for his chivalry
And said she would be fine.
The sight had been too much for her
And that was a thin line.

Though once she had composed herself
She said she'd need some time.
There'd been little left to work with
And this more than a crime.

A STATE OF SHOCK

The city faced a state of shock
Now murders numbered two.
Which had found some people saying
The Mayor had no clue.

Though this time the girl was homeless
It had no less effect.
The populace had grown alarmed
What it could next expect.

Though there had not yet grown panic
It would be soon to come.
For the murders were unnerving
And hard to overcome.

He wished to get ahead of it
Before it hit the news.
He needed to allay the fear
Before panic ensues.

The Mayor held a press briefing
To state what he had known.
The murders had been similar
But reasons were unknown.

ONCE AGAIN

Once again there were no suspects
Because they'd found no clues.
Though Matt thought it impossible
That was the awful news.

The aggravation welled in him
Until he thought he'd scream.
For this had been reality
And not some hellish dream.

Nothing linked Michelle to Meghan
So far as Matt could see.
When it suddenly had hit him
What it could, maybe, be.

The only commonality
That Matt had come to see
Was that both of them were homeless
Or had appeared to be.

In retrospect, Matt could now see
It's homeless she'd appear.
For she would sleep on a park bench
Till next party drew near.

Perhaps they had been targeted.
It's rare homeless were missed.
They're the dregs of society
That often were dismissed.

THE PHONE CALL

The Chief took it upon himself
To make the fateful call.
He recognized they needed help
Or they may lose it all.

He spoke to the Academy
Though no one was to know
That it was he who made the call
Or badly it may go.

The Chief asked for the director
Whose name, they said, was Chad.
Then explained the situation
Which had turned pretty bad.

Chad said an anthropologist
Had been available.
The Chief said he'd take any help
If they were capable.

Chad said that he'd send him tonight
To arrive in the morn.
When the Chief said in all fairness
The man he'd need to warn.

THE ANTHROPOLOGIST

Blake was an anthropologist
They'd chosen to call in.
There had been facts that they had hid
That never should have been.

And Matt had been who greeted Blake
The minute Blake arrived.
Matt first thanked Blake for any help
That Blake may yet provide.

Police, Blake found, were at a loss
To explain what occurred.
They feared the deaths were serial
From what they had inferred.

Each body had been disemboweled
And entrails never found.
Though they'd searched the perimeter
With aid of a bloodhound.

They hoped that Blake could shed some light
To what they were to face.
For up to now they had no clue
What they were meant to chase.

Blake had told them that he needed
To see where this occurred.
Perhaps he'd see what they could not
Though that was not assured.

When Blake's party had first arrived
The first thing Blake had seen.
Was how close in proximity
The homeless to the scene.

Blake's party then approached the camp
To see if any there
Had seen something unusual
Of which they weren't aware.

THE COMMUNITY

Matt said a small community
That Gail had overseen.
To Blake they seemed a sorry lot
Who'd been caught in-between.

Old George was quite the character
Though sadness lived within.
For when his wife had passed away
His kids wouldn't take him in.

Marie was a true bag lady
As all she'd ever own
She carried in a paper bag
She never left alone.

Darlene had been a runaway
Whose destiny was fame
But competition had been stiff
With regrets that she came.

Poor Anna was a mental case
Mistakenly set free.
The world that she was living in
Defied reality.

Blaze use to be a stunt woman
Who was tops in her field.
Until the tragic accident
And career had to yield.

Of course, there also had been Sarge.
The wily veteran.
Who watched over all the others
He saw as companion.

But Gail had seemed to care for them
As if they were her own.
And it had been quite clear to Blake
The compassion she'd shown.

THE INTRODUCTION

A social worker named Gail Kent
Had helped them in their plight.
She spent her days dispensing food
But never spent the night.

When Blake was introduced to Gail
He clearly had been shocked.
For she was not what he'd expect
While eyes upon her locked.

Blake had heard some stories of her
For she had been well-known.
Most had said she was an angel
Through her compassion shown.

Blake thought Gail was too beautiful
To throw her life away.
Believing she may be the key
To how they'd find their way.

URBAN LEGEND

Blake told Gail that their encampment
Was too close to the park.
For something evil lurked within
Which was extremely dark.

Although Gail had heard the legend
She doubted it was true.
For she had seen no evidence
That served to change her view.

Blake then told her it's not legend
That had sparked his concern.
But something evil was at work
That seemed to be nocturne..

PAST HISTORY

Blake saw the way Matt looked at her
And knew there's history.
Though they both had seemed uneasy
Which had been clear to see.

Blake had no wish to get involved
Or come between the two.
He was there to give assistance
And all he wished to do.

Though he thought Gail was attractive,
The one thing he'd not need
Was some troubled relationship
In which he'd intercede.

Whatever problems they may have
Blake would not interfere.
The murders were his lone concern
And reason he was here.

THE SHELTERS

Blake asked Gail why the encampment
When shelters were in place.
Where Gail had quickly turned to him
As anger marred her face.

The shelters, Gail said, were a joke
As they had been unsafe.
For people were attacked at night
And no one there felt safe.

The little that they had possessed
Had been subject to theft.
And when to workers they'd complain,
The workers had turned deaf.

Gail knew of women who were raped
And beatings were not rare.
The streets had seemed a safer place
Though no one there would care.

For though complaints were always filed
They fell upon deaf ears.
The homeless were not powerful
And thus, had sparked no fears.

There would be no repercussions
If pleas they'd fail to heed.
For the homeless were not voters
So, none had seen the need.

THE MEDIA'S ALLEGATIONS

The media had been obsessed
With what police had found.
It knew some facts had been withheld
On which they'd not expound.

It then levied allegations
That the police had lied.
For there were facts they'd not disclosed
As though something to hide.

The media did not accept
Police hands had been tied.
The people had a right to know
The media had cried.

They had a killer in their midst
They'd not identified.
But the clues they had uncovered
They'd clearly chose to hide.

Police feared if the media
Had known what they'd conceal
In their righteous indignation
Each clue they would reveal.

MAXWELL BIRCH

Maxwell Birch was a reporter
Who could not be deterred.
His motto was to find the truth
If it was not conferred.

The precinct that he frequented
Despised him beyond hate.
Because some stories that he wrote
Freed guilty from their fate.

He believed he's a crusader
As one who lived apart.
But in truth he was misguided
Who'd been a bleeding heart.

The information he obtained
He thought produced a clue
To what the true identity
Of whom justice was due.

As Birch was walking home that nigh
He happened by the park.
He never saw his assailant
As it was well past dark.

When Birch was found the next morning
He had been ripped apart.
The only organ left behind
Had been his bleeding heart.

Despite their presence had increased
Police were at a loss
To how Birch had been victimized
Or who'd he'd come across.

And thus, police found victim three
Which now seemed serial.
As all of them were ripped apart
Which was material.

THE ABNORMALITY

There was an abnormality
Was what Amy had said.
After Matt and Blake got to her
When they heard Maxwell's dead.

There was a diff'rence that she found
Between the girls and him.
The girls were both left cavities;
Which in itself was grim.

Unlike the other tragedies
The heart was left behind.
She'd found that fact significant
And almost blew her mind.

The heart should be the first to go
If death by predator.
And yet, she found it still in place
Which she would underscore.

It's possible the heart diseased
But to that can't attest.
Until the lab she had returned
Where she could run a test.

She told them she would know much more
Once autopsy's complete.
And with results she promised them
She'd be more than discrete.

Blake thought he saw a special glance
That passed between the two.
But he could have been mistaken
After all they'd been through.

THE MEDIA BESIDE ITSELF

The media caught wind of Birch
And knew of his demise.
Again, police would not discuss
Whatever they'd surmise.

The media beside themselves
As Birch was one of them.
He had not been that popular
But still they grieved for him.

The media claimed the police
Were ineffectual.
And claimed the people placed at risk
As they weren't factual.

The Mayor, too, responsible
For all that had occurred.
As he had been the one in charge
While evil had endured.

He needed to accept the fact
A coverup occurred.
And he had been responsible
As it he'd not deterred.

THE ALBATROSS

Gail stood in front of City Hall
And screamed in her dismay.
The people in authority
Had looked the other way.

Gail demanded of the Mayor
That shelter he provide.
For all the homeless were at risk
And facing genocide.

But that already was in place
The Mayor had replied.
If they would not avail themselves
They can't say he'd not tried.

The homeless were an albatross
The Mayor had abhorred.
They'd squat on public property
And laws simply ignored.

Those whose lives abstained from purpose
And knew no sense of grace.
While most possessed a troubled past
The rest, a mental case.

Though Blake thought Gail a bleeding heart
With no pragmatic sense,
He admired her dedication
And rose to her defense

Blake interjected, "That's not true."
Then got in Murphy's face.
For his treatment of the homeless
Was truly a disgrace.

The homeless advocates were right.
The Mayor was at fault.
He never used his resources
To deal with each assault.

As Murphy showed a disregard
For each report received.
As he thought he'd all the answers
And nothing else believed.

The Mayor grew apoplectic
So great had been his rage.
Where he had turned away from Blake
To Gail, again, engage.

Murphy was sick of their demands
When no taxes were paid.
And he felt no obligation
To support choices made.

The services provided them
Should be more than enough.
If they did not avail themselves
Then that was simply tough.

He saw no need to shelter those
He knew would run away.
Because none of them were stable
He knew that none would stay.

The taxpayers would foot the bill
For what would go unused.
And he despised the advocates
Who reason had refused.

THE MAYOR'S OUTRAGE

The Mayor had been furious
With allegations made.
In light of what he'd given them
He felt he was betrayed.

The Mayor then fired back at them
They're reckless in their charge.
His job was not providing facts
To anyone at large.

How was it they would dare assume
They had a right to know
Whatever clues police had found
And secrecy forgo?

The Mayor found he was outraged
They placed the blame on him.
As he claimed his prime objective
Was taking care of them.

BLAKE'S THEORY

When Blake and Matt met with the Chief
Blake said that he believed
The homeless had been targeted
Though why he'd not conceived.

The homeless were such easy prey
And there were few who'd care.
Whatever fate awaited them
The public unaware.

The Chief then asked how he'd explain
Why Birch was also killed.
For he clearly was not homeless
And yet, his blood was spilled.

True Birch had not fit the theory
Unless it had been true.
He'd found out the identity
And of it someone knew.

Birch had bragged that he had answers
Which soon he would reveal.
Perhaps that was the impetus
Where death was a done deal.

There was a need to speak with Gail
But Blake would go alone.
For Matt possessed some history
Where some tension was shown.

He needed to confirm the fact
That Birch had nosed around.
Where someone from the homeless camp
May know what Birch had found.

Once their meeting had concluded
Blake pulled Matt to the side.
For something clearly bothered him
Blake could no longer hide.

Blake then asked Matt if he and Gail
Were still somewhat involved.
But Matt told Blake that ship had sailed
And issues were resolved.

SUSPENSION OF THE AUDIT

In light of the emergency
The audit made to halt.
All resources had been applied
To finding who's at fault.

Corruption had been pushed aside
Amidst the killing spree.
The people's safety a concern
To which most would agree.

All resources directed towards
Who was responsible.
Which with the lack of evidence
May be impossible.

But for, at least, the near future
The audit was on hold.
Though guaranteed it would resume
When murders were controlled.

THE HOMELESS CAMP

It was strange what he'd not noticed
As he'd been there before.
Perhaps it's only Gail he'd seen,
Just her and nothing more.

The smell was truly horrible
As they're the great unwashed.
If cleanliness were next to God
These angels had been squashed.

The boxes and the make-shift tents
Were where they chose to dwell.
It was a bleak community
Just one step above hell.

In their struggle for survival
Some lived a fantasy.
Though from drugs or mental illness
Was difficult to see.

The refuse of society
Who're abandoned as prey.
While those assigned to care for them
Had looked the other way.

They all had stories of their own
That led them to this fate.
Though some, it seemed, were victimized
Others would just stagnate.

If all lives mattered why were they
Abandoned to their fate?
When those who held authority
Were facing a stalemate.

GAIL'S REJECTION

Gail pretended not to see him
As Blake walked up to her.
She had a feeling what's to come
And wanted to deter.

Though when Blake asked her to dinner
Gail graciously declined.
For her work consumed her life and
Not socially inclined.

Blake said that he deserved a chance
To which Gail had replied
There're plenty fishes in the sea
Where his charms could be plied.

Blake said it's her he wished to know
And wanted just a chance
To show her who he really was.
Not promising romance.

But Gail refused to change her mind
Where all that Blake could say
Had any of her homeless group
Known Birch to pass this way?

BLAKE'S VISITS

As Blake's visits grew commonplace
Gail had grown more annoyed.
While some had come to welcome him
It's nothing Gail enjoyed.

For she believed they were a ruse
So, he'd stay close to her.
Where maybe he could wear her down
Till he, she would prefer.

Perhaps his visits were sincere
But Gail was full of doubt.
She had no clue to who he was
And feared he was a lout.

He was almost like a stalker
How often he would show.
Although he mostly talked with Sarge
And then he'd up and go.

Perhaps rejection new to him
He found hard to accept.
She'd showed no interest in him
Which he did not expect.

And she had found him awful rude
As to her rarely spoke.
But she could tell he's tempting her
Though she found it no joke.

REVIVAL OF THE LEGEND

The media got wind of it
And legend had revived.
But gave no reasons it believed
Such creatures had survived.

The legend was a proven hoax
But that they'd not report.
Instead, they chose to fuel the fear
Where to the tale resort.

The legend said they're humanoid
But no one had been sure.
Although there had been witnesses
Their observations poor.

The reports were that they surfaced
Within the dead of night.
Where those who had encountered them
Were overwhelmed with fright.

They're dwellers of the underground
Or so, the legends said.
Where most who had encountered them
Had next day been found dead.

Though for years they had not surfaced.
Perhaps they've now returned.
For with changes to the climate
To their old ways had turned.

Their circulation had increased
And ratings were sky high.
The stories of the demantoids
What people wished to buy.

TOO FEARFUL TO EXPRESS

Gail found she's fearful to express
What lurked within her heart.
Not knowing what his feelings were,
She'd not known where to start.

He'd proven a courageous man
Who was good looking, too.
A man possessing principles
That he believed were true.

She'd known that he'd shown interest
Though she'd pushed it aside.
Perhaps because she was afraid
Of what she'd felt inside.

He'd worked his way into her heart
While she was unaware
How much he'd come to mean to her
Where now she'd come to care.

THE THOUGHTS

With all that had been going on
Blake felt somewhat ashamed.
The case he should be working on
But Gail his mind had claimed.

He found it hard to concentrate
On something else but her.
And feared that clues he may have missed
As he felt feelings stir.

It's like a spell was placed on him
That seemed to hold his mind.
For even in his dreams he found
That for Gail he had pined.

He tried to force the thoughts away
But found little success.
For thoughts of Gail kept creeping in
As though to now obsess.

THE URBAN MYTH

The urban legend was a myth,
Or so, the Mayor said.
Through all the years that he had served
Some homeless were found dead.

But in each case the circumstance
Was easily explained.
From exposure to the weather
To anger uncontained.

Police had found no evidence
Such creatures may exist.
So, stories from the media
The people should resist.

There're no such things as demantoids
The Mayor had proclaimed.
These were just unfounded rumors
The media had claimed.

BLAKE AND SARGE

Though Blake spoke to each one of them
It's Sarge who most impressed.
The rest would not acknowledge him
But Sarge questions addressed.

Blake found that he was drawn to Sarge
As he had seen it all.
Though most were secrets he'd conceal
Not wishing to recall.

Yet, most of what he spoke about
Had been life on the street.
How bitter were the coldest nights
And search for food to eat.

But his service was off limits
With no wish to recall
The things that he had seen and done
As he had done it all.

Blake had started to annoy Gail
The way he hung around.
It seemed that he and Sarge grew close
Where Sarge a friend had found.

WANTING TO BE NOTICED

Now wanting Blake to notice her
Gail feared she was too late.
Whether fear or indecision
That made her hesitate.

She knew she'd made mistakes before,
So, this was nothing new.
She let her fear dictate to her
The course she would pursue.

She now regretted she had doubts
And, thus, had failed to act.
She found that she was drawn to him
And that was just a fact.

But she found her indecision
On which she had relied.
Had cost her what she truly wished
Which now may be denied.

RECONSIDERATION

Gail saw the others trusted him
So, why was she the one
Who'd chosen to be hesitant
As trust in him she'd none.

Her instinct to protect herself
But now, she thought from what?
It's a dinner invitation
Not some ungodly plot.

She thought that Blake had made a point
That he deserved a chance.
But then why had she denied him
By sticking to her stance?

Although the opportunity
May now have slipped away.
Gail still had felt the need to try
And somehow save the day.

When Gail had first walked up to him
It caught Blake by surprise.
He wondered what he'd wrongly done
For which she'd now chastise.

But Gail said she'd reconsidered
When giving it some thought.
Was the invitation open
Or was this all for naught?

Blake then stammered it was open.
She'd be ready at eight.
But just to make it very clear
This would not be a date!

FRIEND REQUEST

Marie one day came up to Blake
And asked to be his friend.
There really had been no one else
On whom she could depend.

She'd seen that he'd grown close to Sarge
And Sarge she thought okay.
She never had a friend before
Though why she would not say.

She looked at him with pleading eyes
Afraid Blake would say no.
But Blake's heart had gone out to her
In ways she could not know.

Blake said of course he'd be her friend
And honored that she asked.
Which caused Marie to brightly smile
With joy that went unmasked.

Gail saw there was a side to Blake
That she liked very much.
For she had watched it all unfold
And loved his gentle touch.

AT DINNER

At dinner both felt ill at ease
Though neither had known why.
For Gail declared it was no date
So, neither should felt shy.

After they'd eaten Blake asked Gail
What was it he had done
That had led her to mistrust him
Cause clue he had was none.

He had only wished to know her
And for her to know him.
But he recognized some issues
Clearly divided them.

Gail had not wished to speak of it
And made that very clear,
Then Blake had said he cared for her
And reason he was here.

If she thought she could not trust him
Then why had she agreed
To accept his invitation
Except she'd felt some need?

If she had found she could not trust
Then he would walk away.
Although he must admit to her
He really wished to stay.

Blake thought that Gail had looked distressed
Which he'd not meant to do.
Then looked as though she may break down
If this path he'd pursue.

Blake told her he apologized
As he was out of line.
If secrets she felt she must keep
To him that would be fine.

GAIL'S STORY

When Gail was young, she made mistakes
Because she had been wild.
Where the result of an affair
Was she had borne a child.

The father swore to stand by her
But then he disappeared.
Where she was left alone and scared
With child that must be reared.

She'd found that she was overwhelmed
So, to the church she'd turned.
The church had chose to take them in
Though redemption not earned.

The church then claimed the child as theirs
While she was cast aside.
Because the child was born of sin,
Which it would not abide.

Years later she returned to church
In hope she could reclaim
The child that she had given up
And never gave a name.

But found the child was long since gone
And church refused to trace.
Now for the child she'd given up
She suffered in disgrace.

So, her life she dedicated,
Redemption to attain.
Although nothing she accomplished
Relieved her of her pain.

Though trust issues were a result
Of those mistakes she made.
It could have been a whole lot worse
Than penalty she paid.

CAUGHT OFF GUARD

The knock had caught Gail by surprise
As it was not yet dawn.
But when the door she threw open
Matt stood on her front lawn.

Another victim had been found
They'd not identified.
Matt wanted Gail to go with him,
If she would be allied.

He knew she worked with many groups
And had known most by name.
Matt hoped she could identify
Whatever they should claim.

Gail really had no wish to go
But if Matt turned to her.
He really must be desperate
If favor he'd incur.

The sight had almost made her sick
As it was ripped apart.
Where it barely had looked human
But more like abstract art.

She studied it the best she could
But said she was not sure.
It may have been a guy she knew
But that she'd not assure.

Matt then thanked her for her efforts
He knew it would be rough.
But in light of the circumstance
He knew that she was tough.

WORDS OF COMFORT

On one visit Sarge had asked Blake
If they should be concerned.
The park was just a block away
And bad things of it learned.

Sarge had worried that the others
May somehow be at risk.
For they'd receive no protection
As they're an asterisk.

Sarge simply wished to be prepared
If something should occur.
He'd felt a need to watch o'er them
Where safety he'd assure.

Then Blake told Sarge what he believed
Was once it had grown dark
That none of them should ever get
Too close to that damn park.

Though Sarge had sighed as if relieved
Blake could still plainly see
His words had not been comforting
As he'd hoped they would be.

A GROWING PROBLEM

The protests grew in frequency
And so had their demands.
While Gail was at the heart of it
And giving the commands.

She really had become a pain
That he could not ignore.
She was a threat to his regime
He'd no longer stand for.

But she was in the public's eye
And a hero to some.
She seemed to be untouchable
As martyr she'd become.

But there had to be an answer
To somehow neutralize
The influence that Gail possessed
That Murphy did despise.

Gail had grown to be a problem
With which he'd have to deal.
For he had thought it obvious
His limelight sought to steal.

THE ALTERCATION

The cop had tried to make them move
When Gail had interfered.
They had not bothered anyone
She cried as she had teared.

The cop then punched her in the face
Which took her off her feet.
Then Blake decided to step in
To challenge, though discrete.

But there could be no reasoning
With one so full of hate.
Who next had took a swing at Blake
Though Blake ignored the bait.

The cop was then beside himself
So great had grown his rage.
He pulled his gun for an arrest
Which Blake tried to downstage.

When in the heat of the moment
The gun simply misfired.
Next Blake had grabbed his abdomen
And to the ground retired.

He fought to retain consciousness
Although the strain was great.
Gail's voice had seemed some miles away
While pain would not abate.

Though her touch was oddly soothing,
He still had felt the pain.
He saw she tried to stop the flow
But rapid grew the stain.

When he awoke Gail had been there
Asleep by his bedside.
The nurse who came to check on him
Said she'd not left his side.

The cop they heard was disciplined
But badge had been retained.
He'd claimed it was an accident
And actions were restrained.

RESPONSE TO THE INCIDENT

The Mayor at his news briefing
Had mentioned the assault
And said the homeless advocate
Had been the one at fault.

He further said the incident
Was of no real concern.
It simply was an accident
As far as they'd discern.

The officer had been attacked
Though it was unprovoked.
Where it had been in his defense
Violence was invoked.

The Mayor said he'd been assured
That when this went to trial
The woman who's responsible
Would be shown to be vile.

The Mayor said he's confident
That justice would be done.
Although the Mayor seemed surprised
That Blake had been the one.

From information he received
The culprit was female.
The Mayor, thus, had been surprised
In light of this detail.

Although it made no difference
As far as he's concerned.
The perpetrator had been caught
And punishment well earned.

RECOVERY

Gail sat and watched him lying there
Though for now he's alive.
But the doctors were uncertain
If he'd, somehow, survive.

She prayed to God he would survive
But held out little hope.
The medics said he twice had died
But both times they could cope.

Blake woke to find Gail by his bed
Though pain was not bereft.
The nurse that came to check on him
Said Gail had never left.

When Gail awoke. Matt was awake.
So, Gail tossed him a smile.
Then she asked him how he's feeling
Where grin Blake tried to dial.

He found that he could barely speak
But wanted Gail to know
How much he did appreciate
She would not let him go.

Gail then softly touched his forehead
As words she could not find.
While he had slept, she studied him
As he'd been on her mind.

Her touch had sent a thrill though him
Like none he'd known before.
And in her eyes he thought he saw
What he'd been hoping for.

The doctors said recovery
Would take a little time.
His blood loss was significant
And he'd have hills to climb.

THE CHARGES

Police arrived at Blake's bedside
To tell him he'd been charged
Of assaulting an officer
When he would be discharged.

Gail claimed this was a travesty
As that had not been true.
The officer assaulted Blake
And also struck her, too.

The officers just shrugged and left
As though not their concern.
In shock, Gail turned to look at Blake
And felt her anger churn.

For Blake had very nearly died
Due to the cop's rampage.
And now to find that Blake was charged
Was clearly an outrage.

Gail retained for Blake a lawyer
She thought was very good.
Who had listened to their story
And would do what he could.

ON EXIT FROM RECOVERY

As Blake had left recovery
Matt happened to stop by.
He was the bearer of bad news
And had no wish to lie.

Another homeless man was killed.
Though one Gail had not known.
While the details had been sketchy,
A pattern clearly shown.

Again, the man was ripped to shreds
As though killed by a beast.
His body had been disemboweled
As if there'd been a feast.

Matt said that Amy was distraught
As she'd found once again
That there was nothing she could glean
From state that he'd been in.

This attack had been more brazen
And yet, they'd still no clue
To who or what they're dealing with
Which had been nothing new.

THE MAGISTRATE

Following his recovery
Blake found he had been charged
For assaulting an officer
While duties he discharged.

Blake stood before the magistrate
And said he would accept
Whatever was the punishment
For fighting the inept.

The officer had started it
Flaunting authority.
Those people had done nothing wrong
But he'd not leave them be.

Because it was his first offense,
The magistrate ordained
He'd be assigned public service
And would not be detained.

And since the homeless were the cause
That led to his arrest.
He'd be assigned to help Gail Kent
Based mainly on request.

He also had released Blake from
His contract with police.
They could not have a contractor
Who failed to keep the peace.

A MISTAKE IN JUDGMENT

Matt found Blake to say he's sorry
For news had traveled fast.
Matt thought the ruling was unfair
And had left him aghast.

For all had known the cop had lied
As he had history.
There'd been a number of complaints.
Suspensions numbered three.

They thought he was a dirty cop
But nothing had been proved.
The Mayor's office was a friend
As he'd not been removed.

There was no justice to be served
As once again he'd skate.
While Blake was left to agonize
Why this had been his fate.

Matt told him he would be in touch
If Matt found something new.
The judge had made a huge mistake
That now he can't undo.

THE PROVOCATION

One day in Blake's recovery
Gail took him for fresh air.
Though he was not opposed to it
He did not seem to care.

Gail said a penny for his thoughts
As Blake looked miles away.
He said to Gail he'd been setup.
At least, it looked that way.

For all the time he'd been with her
No cop ever before
Had even asked for them to move
Until there came this bore.

It had been a conspiracy
If Gail would just reflect.
The cop was argumentative
More than one would expect.

GORDON BOSTIC

It was as though he'd provoked him
To give him an excuse
To create a situation
In which he could cut loose.

It likely was no accident
But something that was planned.
Maybe he'd discovered something
For which he would be damned.

Although he had no idea
What someone thought he'd known
But what had been a mystery
He had no wish to own.

PANIC GRIPPED THE CITY

Although panic gripped the city
It was somewhat controlled.
For it mainly seemed the homeless
Were whom the killer trolled.

However now with Maxwell's death
A new sense of alarm
That no one was completely safe
Nor immunized from harm.

The Mayor made assurances
That no one had believed.
He said he had control of it
But no support received.

Murphy claimed he'd taken measures
So, safety was assured.
Police presence had been increased
And park had been secured.

Then Murphy blamed the residents
As alerts were ignored.
While policies he put in place
Had all gone unexplored.

But his leadership was questioned
As fear had hold of them.
For as they saw the death count rise
They had lost faith in him.

WHAT BLAKE LEARNED FROM PUBLIC SERVICE

He'd never known someone before
So, all in for a cause.
It was almost blind devotion
She offered without pause.

Gail had tried to bring attention
To what had been their plight.
But ev'ryone turned a blind eye,
Out of mind, out of sight.

Gail found no time for anything
Beyond what was her cause.
For her people had need of her
Despite weakness and flaws.

She was committed to her cause
For which she firmly stood.
Though Blake doubted that the homeless
Had ever understood.

Though Blake found she was relentless
And could not be deterred.
She was awash in compassion
Which she'd gladly conferred.

Blake wanted Gail to notice him
But he had not known how.
For he'd never been enamored
As much as he was now.

IN NEED OF A LIBATION

Matt met Blake for drinks one night
As both were at a loss
To explain what was happening
Or what they'd come across.

Matt thought it very curious
That no one saw or heard
Anything involved with murder.
Which Matt thought was absurd.

For there had to be a struggle
As, surely, they'd fought back.
There was no one who'd just stand there
While they're under attack.

While Blake agreed it made no sense.
The facts were what they were.
And with no shred of evidence
There's little to infer.

There was something that they're missing
But neither had a clue.
Though perhaps one more libation
Will help them think things through.

When suddenly Matt's phone had rung
Though conversation brief.
Matt said they'd found another one
But this one may bring grief.

MARIE'S ABDUCTION

They heard the box be ripped apart
And then they heard the scream.
It was too dark to clearly see
But this had been no dream.

They huddled in their make-shift homes
In fear they would be next.
And there were none that they could call
Or even try to text.

It had only taken minutes
Although it seemed like days.
The terror unmistakable
In all too many ways.

Next morning when they dared emerge
They found Marie was gone.
The box that she was living in
Crushed as though sat upon.

Police discovered what was left
Of what was once Marie.
It had not been a pretty sight
And had been hard to see.

What's left hard to identify
As what it once had been.
But, luckily, they found her head
Though bad state it was in.

Again, there was no evidence
To what or whom to blame.
For the homeless seemed a target
That something found fair game.

Perhaps Michelle was a mistake
And misidentified.
If she'd been sleeping on a bench
When she, the perp had spied.

Blake told police keep Gail away
So, she'd not have to see
What once had been a friend of hers
They thought may be Marie.

BLAKE WENT TO CHECK ON THEM

Blake found that they were terrified
When he'd gotten to them.
Even Sarge, it seemed, was shaken
As all eyes turned to him.

They had all survived a nightmare
Of which they would not speak.
For all of them could still recall
The horror in her shriek.

Blake saw the terror in their eyes
As they were so exposed.
After all, they were the homeless
Who're easily disposed.

It seemed that Blaze was traumatized
As she just sat and stared.
And completely unresponsive
To anyone who cared.

Blake found his heart went out to them
With little he could do.
Unless he chose to stay with them
And thus, be homeless too.

GAIL'S GRIEF

Gail screamed that Blake's responsible
And she held him to blame.
He'd led them all to trust in him
And thus, he bore the shame.

She slammed her fists into his chest
And then broke down and cried.
Her grief was inconsolable
No matter how he tried.

She screamed at him to get away
For with him she was through.
She'd dared to place her trust in him
To find it was not due.

She'd no desire to be with him
As he had proved a fraud.
The way he'd turned his back on them
Had proven he was flawed.

Blake knew that grief was driving her
And he had felt her pain.
But he was not responsible
As he'd nothing to gain.

He knew it's grief that she expressed
Though some things had been true.
For he had made them promises
But had not followed through.

He told Sarge to look after her
As he had to return.
To look for any evidence
And see what he could learn.

UNDER FIRE

While the Mayor seethed with anger
He saw the protests grow.
He knew who was behind it all
And pledged she had to go.

For they'd become an annoyance
The Mayor did not need.
For he was under constant fire
That warnings he'd not heed.

They chanted he should be removed
Because he'd never cared.
Their plight had been of no concern
To one so richly heired.

Murphy felt no sense of justice
Refusing to protect
The ones who're most vulnerable
And chosen to neglect.

The Mayor seethed in his disgust
Of what they could not see.
The homeless were a constant drain
On their community.

DAZED AND CONFUSED

As he'd driven to the crime scene
He was dazed and confused.
How was it he's responsible
For how she'd been abused?

Gail's strength of faith Blake had admired
So, it was a surprise
How quickly she had turned on him
After Marie's demise.

Her accusations hit him hard
And cut him to the core.
Perhaps it was her grief talking.
Perhaps it's something more.

He'd not believe that she believed
That he was capable
Of wishing any of them harmed
Which was not plausible.

He guessed she had not known him well,
Or known him well enough.
If she had thought him capable
Of having been that tough.

BLAKE'S FRUSTRATION

When Blake returned Amy was there
Though said she had no clue.
Her death was more than similar
And she'd found nothing new.

Because he cared so much for Gail
He came to care for them.
To Gail they were like family
Though none of them a gem.

And now to find Marie was dead
Had drove him to the brink.
This nightmare may not have an end,
He had begun to think.

Blake then cursed in his frustration
And felt his anger swell.
Gail thought he was responsible
And now he did as well.

He was asked here as an expert
But as that he had failed.
The murders still had been unsolved,
Against which he had railed.

The woman that he'd come to love
Now showered him with blame.
Where even if she could forgive
May never be the same.

NO TAKING BACK

While Gail's grief impaired her judgment
And caused her to lash out.
Where now that she had calmed herself
Regretted what she'd spout.

She knew she'd said some hurtful things
Which truly were not fair.
And Blake had took the brunt of it
Because he had been there.

She feared there was no taking back
The awful things she'd said.
The look that Blake had given her
Still echoed in her head.

She needed to apologize
But phone calls he ignored.
She feared that he was furious
Or she he now abhorred.

She prayed the he had understood
That was not really her.
It was her grief that was exposed
To which she would defer.

A STRANGER NO MORE

Blake was brooding in the darkness
When the doorbell had rung.
He started not to answer it
For Marie's death still stung.

The door he opened to find Gail
Who asked if she'd come in.
She said that she'd tried to call him
And wondered where he'd been.

Gail started to turn on a light
When Blake said leave it dark.
Although he'd been prohibited
He still had searched the park.

She's not the woman that he thought
To have lashed out that way.
He, too, had felt the pangs of grief
That Marie passed away.

Gail wanted to apologize
But Blake had said no need.
The more he thought of what she said
The more he had agreed.

Gail told him that it had been her
Who this time had been wrong.
The accusations that she made
Had all been way too strong.

She thought it was the shock of it
That caused her to react.
She knew he's not responsible
And that she wished back tracked.

Then she asked for his forgiveness
As he had claimed her heart.
She had never wished to hurt him
Though what she said not smart.

Blake saw the tears well in her eyes
And could not turn away.
For she had claimed his heart as well
Which he had yet to say.

He took her in his arms and said
That he had loved her, too.
And in the darkness of the night
Had proven it was true.

She had come to him a stranger
Who wanted to be more.
Where night brought opportunity
That love they could explore.

WITNESSES

The media found witnesses
That claimed that they had seen
The creatures of the underworld
That were vicious and mean.

But their stories had seemed rehearsed
As though they had been paid.
For that to which they testified
Had seemed to be replayed.

With fangs and claws they disemboweled
Whomever they could find.
And never was there mercy shown
As to it they were blind.

Each presented to the Mayor
As though their stories fact.
To where the Mayor was resolved
Upon this he must act.

The evidence was crystal clear
Though it police denied.
For it all had matched the legend
Which proved police had lied.

The Mayor, though, became convinced
The legend had been true.
And had now clearly resurfaced
To reign terror anew.

Matt thought it's clear each one was coached.
With each account the same.
There had been phrases they'd repeat
As each had made their claim.

Matt had wondered where they found them
As they took time to look.
But had no one who was willing
Or had exception took.

So, Matt had found it curious
The media had found
A group they claimed were witnesses
To on this tale expound.

Despite the media reports
Matt found he disagreed
With their claims that there were creatures
Who surfaced just to feed.

Matt thought the Mayor ill informed
If this he'd entertain.
For a con was perpetrated
And thought that very plain.

Although Matt found he must admit
From what the people knew.
How people may come to conclude
The legend had been true.

WANTING NOTHING MORE

Blake studied ev'rything she did
As breakfast she prepared.
He feared he'd never find the words
To say how much he cared.

The evening was more magical
Than he would have believed.
And proved there was much more to her
Than he'd ever perceived.

He'd not known that he'd been looking
Until it's Gail he'd found.
Where now he would do anything
To ensure she's around.

He'd not known what he was missing
Till Gail had come along.
A woman who's compassionate
Who also had been strong.

He knew his heart belonged to her
With much more to explore.
She now was ev'rything to him
And wanted nothing more.

THE CHIEF'S MEETING WITH THE MAYOR

When the Chief met with the Mayor
It had been to inform
The murders still a mystery
That went beyond the norm.

The murders they could not explain
But all were disemboweled.
And each it seemed was targeted
Before they were befouled.

Police could find no witnesses
Despite how hard they tried.
The coroner was at a loss
To say how they had died.

Though police had called them murders
They'd found nothing to link
The victims or the neighborhoods
To something they could sync.

Murphy asked about the creatures
And if they'd seen a sign
That proved the creatures did exist
And on mankind would dine.

Though through the years there were reports
Such creatures had been spied.
There'd truly been no evidence
To prove they had not lied.

Police had found no evidence
The creatures may exist.
And yet, reports they still received
As rumors did persist.

It was a monster that they sought
Of that Chief had no doubt.
No human could be capable
Of going this all-out,

There're certain inconsistencies
Police could not explain.
The Mayor wished it swept away
And made that very plain.

BREAKFAST TALK

At breakfast Gail had looked at him
But had not said a word.
As though she was afraid to ask
Or thought it was absurd.

Although to him she'd bared her soul,
She'd known little of him.
She thought she had a right to know
Whether it's light or grim.

If they'd wished a relationship
They both must learn to trust.
They had needed to be open
Because she thought they must.

His parents both were maniacs
Who bordered on insane.
His life had been a living hell
Where love he had to feign.

The military his escape
Where he had proudly served.
He had even earned some medals
Though thought them undeserved.

With his enlistment set to end
He had a choice to make.
Which either was to return home
Or greater risks to take.

He went to the Academy
Where his degree he earned.
He found he really liked it there
So, other offers spurned.

He'd never chosen to look back
To where he had come from.
His parents both were maniacs
He'd still not overcome.

His story's not remarkable.
In fact, he thought it bland.
Though Gail had sweetly smiled at him
Then gently kissed his hand.

THE MEDIA'S PROMOTION

The media promoted it
As though it had been fact.
The legend was reality
Upon which they must act.

Relying on their witnesses
They claimed that they could prove
The legend was no fantasy
And it was on the move.

The Mayor ignored evidence
That was as plain as day.
Because the homeless were a blight
He wished would go away.

As long as no real citizens
Had been placed in harm's way.
The Mayor did not give a damn
If some should pass away.

They said it was a tragedy
That he had let occur.
It almost was like ancient Rome
Where terror they'd endure.

A NIGHT OUT

When Gail and Blake entered the pub
They saw Amy and Matt.
Who tried to get their attention
To come sit where they sat.

It seemed like weeks since they'd been out
Though Gail, Matt had to coax.
She'd grown wary of the nighttime
And what the nighttime cloaks.

But he pub that night was crowded
With people of good cheer.
Despite what had been happening
They were not slaves to fear.

While Gail and Amy hit it off
As though they'd been best friends.
For Amy was a fan of Gail
And kept up with her trends.

The evening was a pleasant one
And far removed from death.
It was a night to be enjoyed
And, maybe, catch their breath.

Though Blake was not that good at it
Gail had wanted to dance.
But although he chose to warn her
Gail said she'd take a chance.

Blake thought it nice to see her smile,
For her smiles had been rare.
But in light of the circumstance
There'd been few smiles to spare.

THE MEETING

With the meeting called to order
There're some who were on edge.
For they'd worried what the Mayor
May do to fill his pledge.

The Mayor said it's obvious
What steps they'd need to take.
The tunnels they'd need to explore.
To not, was a mistake.

Though not all were in agreement,
No one expressed dissent.
For the Mayor's associates
Had served at his consent.

So, all the tunnels would be searched
With hope that they could find
The creatures from the underground
Who on their people dined.

THE ACTION PLAN

The Mayor had an action plan
He briefly had disclosed.
He said they'd seen enough of this
Where will would be imposed.

He said he'd organize a search
To seek the creatures out.
The legend said they're underground
Which left him little doubt.

They'd strike at them within their lair
And take them by surprise.
No longer would man be the prey
As it was time to rise.

He placed a call for volunteers
To supplement police.
The task he said was dangerous
But if they wished for peace

There's only one alternative
As far as he could see.
But strike them on their own home turf
When unprepared they'd be.

THE SEARCH

The sewer tunnels were pitch black
And few wished to go in
Not knowing where the tunnels led
Nor what may lurk within.

But Murphy's orders were to search
For what the tunnels hid.
If something truly lived down there
The next step was to rid.

For hours they had trudged through muck
And had waded through slime.
Where many had grown to believe
This was a waste of time.

Yet, the search had proven futile,
It gave them peace of mind.
Although none of them considered
They may be hard to find.

The Mayor found it circumspect
No single clue was found.
For each report that he received
Said they'd lived underground.

And yet, they'd found no evidence
That the creatures exist.
And what about the witnesses
Whose claims would still persist?

The Mayor said they'd take a break
Before the search resumed.
For he had not felt confident
With not a clue exhumed.

Then it came to someone's notice
That all had not returned.
At least one of them was missing
It quickly had been learned.

Each party then took attendance
To find they'd absentees.
And assumed within the tunnels
Discovered the species.

The Mayor was incredulous
That such a thing occurred.
But now he had the evidence
With which most had concurred.

REVIVAL OF THE LEGEND

The media got wind of it
But no one had known how.
police had kept it under wraps
But source they'd disavow.

No one's to know about the search
Except those who're involved.
And they were sworn to secrecy
So, Murphy was absolved.

But they had then revived the tales
That ev'ry child had heard.
Of creatures who lived underground
Against whom they must gird.

It said it's clear that they'd returned
From what the search revealed.
As members of the search parties
Were from their parties peeled.

There's no other explanation,
The media could find,
But that the legend had been true
To which police were blind.

Then the media had questioned
What the Mayor would do
When once he came to recognize
The legend had been true.

THE QUANDARY

The Mayor faced a quandary
Of what he next should do.
Do they return to look for them
Or forfeit a rescue?

With media all over it
The damage had been done.
For, now, they had called him reckless
While nothing had been won.

Although it's they who forced his hand
To that they'd not admit.
For he had been the one in charge
And thus, the cause of it.

The numbers that he sacrificed
Were twice the murder count.
As the search was his idea
And thus, was his to mount.

But the search was a disaster
And the Mayor they blamed.
Although they had demanded it
That fact had gone unclaimed.

SHE'D MADE HERSELF A TARGET

She was constantly complaining
That he'd not done enough.
She said he was a criminal
Whose policies were fluff.

He'd provided no protection
And, thus, they were exposed.
The homeless were a sacrifice
The Mayor had imposed.

The man had been a heartless beast
Who would pretend to care.
But when it came time for action
He never had been there.

Her accusations never stopped
Where she'd become a pain.
As the Mayor felt resentment
He'd found hard to contain.

She had made herself a target
As far as he's concerned.
For she'd become an enemy
Who needed to be turned.

GAIL'S ATTACK

As it was her normal practice
Gail stayed in after dark.
It's rare that she would venture out
Much less go to the park.

But when she saw that Sarge had called
Her interest was piqued.
She'd never known he had a phone
Or on one dared to speak.

For Sarge hated technology
And in it placed no trust.
He only would make use of it
If he had found he must.

The message that was left for her
Gail found to be bizarre.
It told her to come to the park
But not to bring her car.

So, discarding better judgment
Gail headed to the park.
For if it's true that Sarge had called
She'd known it was no lark.

The park at night most would avoid
But there's always a few
Who thought that they were daredevils
Or those who had no clue.

But on that night Gail saw no one
Though it was very dark.
There was no moon to rain some light
Where path she could not mark.

She called for Sarge with no response
Which filled her with some doubt.
Perhaps the message was a prank
Or ruse to lure her out.

Then Gail thought she'd seen movement
But she had not been sure.
The darkness an impediment
Her safety to ensure.

The attack had come from nowhere
And caught her by surprise.
The first blow took her off her feet
Because she'd been unwise.

But she'd been trained in martial arts
And savagely fought back.
She was not a helpless woman
Who'd cave to the attack.

As quickly as it had been launched
The attack seemed to cease.
As though assailant was surprised
And sought its own release.

Though when it seemed that she was safe
She collapsed and then cried.
Because of her own ignorance
She clearly could have died.

The only number on speed dial
Was who she chose to call.
Although when Blake had come to her
Her first response was ball.

Blake held her tightly in his arms
And whispered it's okay.
Whatever had assaulted her
Had simply run away

Gail asked Blake to stay with her
As she was still afraid.
He graciously accepted that
But had no promise made.

When they returned to Gail's abode,
Gail to Blake had confessed
The attack had not been random
As she had been addressed.

For to the park she had been lured
Where she was meant to die.
She clearly had been targeted.
The question had been why.

THE NIGHTMARE HAD TO END

Blake's rage was uncontrollable
When he had heard the news.
So, when he arrived at Matt's house
He'd had a shortened fuse.

Though shocked to find Blake at his door,
Matt asked him to come in.
Then Amy called from the kitchen
To see who it had been.

When Matt replied that it was Blake
She joined them in the room.
As Matt asked Blake what's the matter
Though felt a sense of gloom.

Blake said that Gail had been attacked
As to the park was lured.
Matt asked if Gail had been okay.
Blake said he'd been assured.

Of course, she had been shaken up
So, Blake could not stay long.
But creatures weren't responsible
Of that, belief was strong.

Police were at her house right now.
That's why he chose to leave.
Blake wanted Matt to know the facts
Before twists they could weave.

Blake said this nightmare had to end
And he had made a vow.
He'd be the one responsible
Though right then knew not how.

NOT TO BE DEFIED

He thought he was above reproach
And should not be defied.
Gail had grown to be a nuisance
As patience she had tried.

It seemed that she was ev'rywhere
And had become a pain.
For she would dare to challenge him
Where rage hard to contain.

She'd begun to sway opinion
Which he could not allow.
He'd found the need to silence her
But had not known quite how.

She'd become a public figure
He needed to destroy.
It must be done strategic'ly
So, stealth he must employ.

He thought that once Gail was dismissed
Or was discredited,
The rallies that had hounded him
Would grow more edited.

A RETURN TO THE SCENE

The injuries that Gail received
Had not been that severe.
Blake had said that she was lucky
For what to him was clear

This had not been some random act
That she'd stumbled into.
For someone lured her to the park
Where harm they meant to do.

When Blake returned to Gail's abode
Police had still been there.
They wished to know Gail's enemies.
Blake said none he's aware.

Police returned them to the park
And scene of Gail's attack.
They wanted to replay events
To see what they could track.

Police again had combed the park
But nothing had they learned.
Her attack unlike the others
As from it she returned.

When Matt arrived, he went to Gail
To see if she's okay.
But he also wished her story
As it she would relay.

Gail told Matt she got a phone call
And thought it Sarge's voice.
It asked her to come to the park
Where she thought she'd no choice.

But she found after she arrived
That there was no one there.
Till as she was about to leave
They'd sprung out of thin air.

She had thought they'd wished to kill her
So, she chose to fight back.
In retrospect, it seemed to her
The target of attack.

Police thought it coincidence
But Blake was not that sure.
Too many similarities
For him to just concur.

Blake looked at Matt with questioning
If safety a concern.
When Matt told Blake to stay with her
As they'd much more to learn.

SURVIVOR'S GUILT

Blake had seen Gail had grown pensive
With something on her mind.
He asked her if she wished to talk
But talking she declined.

He'd no wish to be invasive
Though he had been concerned.
It's clear that something bothered her
As he saw her mind churned.

When suddenly she turned to him
And asked if she's to blame.
For most of those who had been killed
She had known them by name.

Blake said it was ridiculous
For her to have believed
That she had any part in what
The fates they had received.

Gail said she'd been an advocate
Who'd come on pretty strong
And she'd ruffled plenty feathers
Of those she thought were wrong.

Perhaps the murders were revenge
For issues she had raised.
She knew she'd made some enemies
Although she had been praised.

Where then the tears began to flow
As her frustration grew.
She could grasp no explanation
Except her guilt was due.

Into his arms she then collapsed
As penance she thought due.
She was the one responsible
And he had known it too.

Blake held her tightly as he could
In hope he'd reassure
She's not the one responsible
Of that he was damn sure.

Blake thought it was survivor's guilt
That had a hold of her.
For of all the gruesome murders
It's death she did defer.

And she'd felt the same frustration
That he, himself, had felt.
With little he could do for her
Which caused his heart to melt.

THE MAYOR'S DAILY BRIEFINGS

His daily briefings were a waste
As he'd say nothing new.
He mainly would defend himself
From criticisms due.

He would charge the allegations
Against him were untrue.
They were simply agitators
Who'd nothing else to do.

He'd claim the efforts that were made
The best that they could do.
Whatever they were dealing with
Had never left a clue.

The situation was not one
Where he'd exert control.
He must allow police to do
Their job and reach their goal.

His heart went out to those who died
But he should not be blamed.
The creatures, he said, would be caught
And justice would be claimed.

Till then it's patience he required
So, justice could be served.
For criticisms he absorbed
Were truly undeserved.

And then he'd give assurances
The city he'd protect.
But most had chosen to believe
The city he'd neglect.

ONE MORNING

One morning when they both arrived
They found that Sarge was gone.
They asked the others where he went
Who'd said he'd just moved on.

Gail then noticed that Sarge's things
Were still where she'd expect.
Which told her that he'd not moved on
For these he'd not neglect.

In panic she had run to Blake
And said there's something wrong.
For Sarge, it seemed, had disappeared
And none knew for how long.

While Blake had said he'd search the streets
Gail had run to the park.
She felt her heart lodge in her throat
As her fear had been stark.

The body Gail had discovered
Had made her gag and puke.
It was an open cavity
Which clearly was no fluke.

Then Blake took Gail into his arms
So, she'd not have to see
What he believed were the remains
Of who Sarge use to be.

Although it was not obvious
Gail knew that it was Sarge.
And as her tears began to flow
Her anger she'd discharge.

The protection she'd requested
They never had received.
The price Sarge paid was ultimate
With safety unachieved.

THEY HAD EACH OTHER

The death of Sarge had hit Gail hard.
More so than had Marie.
For her bond with Sarge was special
Like he was family.

Blake felt the pain as much as Gail
For he'd called Sarge a friend.
His fate was truly undeserved
As was his tragic end.

But at least they had each other
To comfort and console.
Though both had been devastated
Their grief they would control.

There had been no finger pointing
Nor lashing out in pain.
There'd been no wild accusations
As from them they'd abstain.

There had only been the grief
And utter sense of loss.
But at least they had each other
Where love was now the boss.

AMY'S DISCOVERY

Matt led the investigation
Which Blake had thought was good.
For Matt in total confidence
Would do the best he could.

Matt gave Blake his assurances
If anything was found.
He'd find some way to let Blake know
As rules he'd work around.

Though again police were baffled
With no clear place to start.
Again, they found no evidence
Nor wisdom to impart.

There was no more that she could learn
From what little remained.
And Amy had apologized
Although she seemed restrained.

Though she lied her eyes betrayed her
To what she tried to hide.
There had been something that she found
She'd not wished to confide.

When Blake, at last, had cornered her
He got her to confess.
There had been something she had seen
That brought her some distress.

There's not one body. There were two.
And what she thought occurred
Was Sarge had stumbled on something
And to action was spurred.

Perhaps he saw the first attack
And tried to intercede.
But something overpowered him
Where life forced to concede.

Though he had paid a heavy price,
A hero to the end.
For Amy had been positive
The first he tried defend.

THE MISSING ASSOCIATES

The Mayor found protests decreased
Since Gail had been attacked.
Perhaps a message had been sent.
Though claimed not one he'd backed.

But those who worked in City Hall
Had noticed they'd not seen
The Mayor's new associates
Since last week they'd convene.

It was not that any missed them
With most of them afraid.
For there'd been something about them
That on their conscience preyed.

No one had ever trusted them
And to some were suspect.
Where the aura they projected
Was one of no respect.

No one had ever spoke to them
For none knew who they were.
One day they simply had appeared
And looking sinister.

And ev'ryone gave a wide berth
Whenever they'd passed by.
For no one wished to trouble them
Unless a wish to die.

Although now that they'd been absent
Left some to wonder why.
They were always with the Mayor
But left him high and dry.

A HARD FACT TO FACE

They'd found it hard to face the fact
That Sarge was really dead.
Although Amy had confirmed it
No tears had yet been shed.

It all had come as such a shock
They weren't sure how to deal.
They both harbored some resentment
That it had not seemed real.

Although Sarge had been a hero
Who'd fallen on hard times.
He still had been a decent man
Who's guilty of no crimes.

His fate they thought was undeserved
And in truth had been cruel.
That's when the tears began to well
And grief began to rule.

Then Gail gasped in realization
The others may not know
That Sarge would not return to them.
So, to them they must go.

THE TRAUMA OF THE NIGHT BEFORE

The trauma of the night before
Had made her stop and ask.
If she had been the cause of this
That someone would unmask.

Perhaps she'd been too passionate
In what she would request.
Perhaps someone took exception
Believing her a pest.

Perhaps it's her allegations
That had someone upset.
Perhaps it's her expectations
That so far were unmet.

But clearly someone wished her dead
And that was just a fact.
Where if her premise had been true
It's not their final act.

She'd not thought she'd made enemies
But, clearly, that's not true.
For some people tried to kill her
As though they thought it due.

THE DARK DAYS

Blake found sleep to be difficult
With what raced through his mind.
In the fact that Sarge was murdered
And Gail not far behind.

He looked at Gail, who's fast asleep,
And thought what could have been.
If escape was not possible
What state would she be in?

He had thought these were the dark days
With all that had occurred.
Their family was targeted
And grief they had endured.

There seemed no purpose for the deaths,
At least, none he could see.
The people were immobilized
As fear gripped the city.

He prayed this would be over soon
And no more had to die.
These had truly been the dark days
And no one could say why.

SARGE'S TRIBUTE

Sarge's tribute had been touching
And Gail thought well deserved.
For the man had died a hero
Where praise was unreserved.

Though the anger that burned in her
She'd never known before.
But it's not vengeance that she sought.
It had been something more.

Possibly it's vindication
For what they had been through.
Though the Mayor thought them worthless
Gail knew that was not true.

These people deserved dignity
Which they had not received.
Where for people like the Mayor
It had not been achieved.

When Gail at last addressed the crowd
Her emotions spewed out.
When she questioned what the Mayor
Had truly been about.

THROWING MONEY DOWN THE SEWER

When the Mayor heard what she'd said
He nearly lost his mind.
The innuendo she implied
His informant streamlined.

The Mayor was fed up with them,
Especially with Gail.
As they were always complaining
The homeless lived in hell.

These advocates were terrorists
As ransom they'd demand.
No matter what he'd allocate
To them was never grand.

Throwing money down a sewer
Was not a bigger waste
Than what the homeless had received
And then simply defaced.

They'd no desire to change themselves
Though many said they did.
They're a drain upon the city
Of which he would be rid.

If they're looking for charity
There're many to be found.
But government's not one of them
As long as he's around.

For the city had true problems
With which he had to deal.
And homeless he had thought a choice
That only they made real

A REVIEW OF THE FACTS

The phone call came from Amy Lynn
Who said she had some news.
But she'd felt uncomfortable
If the phone had been used.

She told Blake to avoid the morgue
As eyes were ev'rywhere.
Instead, he should come to her house
But do so with great care.

When Blake arrived, he'd been surprised
When Matt opened the door.
He'd thought the call a little strange
As he's involved no more.

The court order prevented him
From playing any part
In the prime investigation
Which he was asked to start.

Then Gail arrived just after Blake
As Amy called her too.
Who thought the four of them had need
The facts they should review.

They gathered in her living room
Where facts they would review.
Perhaps there's something that they missed
Or not known that they knew.

Amy was no fan of Murphy
Who'd been poking around.
And constantly was asking her
What details she had found.

She'd thought his actions curious
And, perhaps, a bit odd.
Why should the Mayor be involved
In knowing where she'd trod?

Why was the park the focal point
Of most of the attacks?
No tunnels had been close to it
And had many drawbacks.

Blake said to accept the premise
The legend had been true.
How did the creatures come and go
Or had the park slipped through?

Though there were a ton of questions,
The answers had been few.
Where nothing that seemed rational
Provided them a clue.

While the murders had been savage,
Amy could not conclude
Whether done by an animal
Or by a depraved dude.

Why only target the homeless
Or who appeared to be?
Except, that is, for Maxwell Birch
With known identity.

A clue may be he was special
As profile did not fit.
Perhaps there's something he had known
And died because of it.

Matt said he would investigate
To see if he could find
Whatever Birch was working on
Or what he'd been assigned.

Meanwhile the others should lay low
Until Matt could discern
If the things that they'd discovered
Was some cause for concern.

THE CHANGE

The city faced an urgency
With which he would not deal.
As though he saw no urgency
Or thought it was not real.

Though he felt the pressure building
To have the murders solved.
Yet, it seemed he was satisfied
They still were unresolved.

As though he'd grown oblivious
To all that had occurred.
For questions they had asked of him
He simply had deferred.

They'd called him irresponsible
But he'd not seemed to care.
Whatever had come over him
No one had been aware.

They'd seen a subtle change in him
That no one could explain.
As though some secret he possessed
No one's to ascertain.

For he had grown more secretive
Than he had ever been.
Which had disrupted City Hall
As to what state he's in.

THE PLAN

Blake thought, perhaps, he had a plan
But not sure it's legit.
For it involved the Thunderbirds
Who'd want no part of it.

For ev'ry night they roamed the park
To drink and raise some hell.
And yet, they had been left alone
As far as Blake could tell.

They claimed they'd never seen a thing
And maybe that was true.
But so far they had been immune
To what the homeless due.

What if they went under cover
In Thunderbird disguise?
In that way they'd have full access
And on the park have eyes.

They would need a pretend victim
For which Gail volunteered.
But Blake was having none of it
And veto engineered.

Perhaps one of the Thunderbirds
They, somehow, could convince.
Maybe someone with a court date
Who's lacking a defense.

Dan Burke had an outstanding charge
And fines he'd yet to pay.
He told them he would volunteer
If both should go away.

Matt had some friends that he could trust
Who're also on the force
And had volunteered to help him
Upon his stated course.

Matt told Blake he could not take part
In what was to occur
With the court order specific
That he could not detour.

AN ISSUE OF TRUST

Though the Chief they thought any ally
How could they know for sure?
For City Hall was full of leaks
That none seemed to censure.

Matt argued that he should be told
As he could offer aid.
But Blake unsure who they could trust
And thus, had been afraid.

The plan Blake would not jeopardize
By spreading it around.
They would need to be selective
If culprit to be found.

But Matt had trusted in the Chief
And thought he should be told.
If nothing else they'd find the truth
If their trust had been sold.

Then Blake replied the body count
Already was too high.
Where any leak would lead to more
Who would be made to die.

This could be a conspiracy,
Though who could say for sure.
The whole thing was a mystery
With no clues to secure.

So, Blake and Matt had both agreed
That secrecy's a must.
Matt said he would inform the Chief
After they made the bust.

THE PLAN IN ACTION

They sat up a surveillance point
Before dusk the next day.
They dressed Dan as a homeless man
With plan well under way.

Matt saw the men enter the park
In stealth to not be seen.
A couple he had thought he'd known
Though from where could not glean.

The men were dressed in plastic suits
That covered head to toe.
Then hid and waited patiently
For some target to show.

When Dan approached their hiding spot
The men rushed to attack.
It caught Dan by complete surprise
Though he tried to fight back.

But before they could strike a blow
Matt's volunteers arrived.
Which had sparked a confrontation
Where caution had nosedived.

Then in all of the confusion
A melee had ensued.
Until Matt and his volunteers
Had all the men subdued.

The implements that they had bore
Had cruelly been designed.
As though for an inquisition
Where torture would be mined.

All of a sudden Blake appeared
Who'd waited for arrest.
He said that he had known the men
And to that would attest.

They're the Mayor's associates
And he could only guess
That they'd done the Mayor's bidding
But needed to confess.

THEIR CONFESSION

In the sum of their confession
Murphy's men had revealed
To how massive the corruption
That Murphy wished concealed.

Where the level of corruption
Had seemed beyond belief.
The former Mayor started it
Although her tenure brief.

While the city reeled in terror,
Murphy had robbed it blind.
Where all he needed was escape
With good life his to find.

For with the audit soon to start
And with the Mayor gone.
That Murphy had grown desperate
That soon they would catch on.

So, he needed a distraction
From audit taking place.
He knew that in the course of time
The money they would trace.

To cover his embezzlement
Some people had to die.
Where revival of the legend
Would mask the reasons why.

That ev'ryone bought into it
Had been a big surprise.
But found to perpetrate the myth
The deaths must scandalize.

Matt looked at Blake and shook his head
How easily they caved.
While admitting to the murders
That had been so depraved.

CONFRONTATION WITH THE MAYOR

When Blake went to see the Mayor
He looked him in the eye.
Blake knew Murphy behind it all
And wanted to know why.

When Murphy in his lone response
Had ev'rything denied.
Blake wished to punch him in the face
Because Blake knew he lied.

But Matt arrived with officers
Where Murphy they'd arrest.
And told him ev'rything he owned
He'd be made to divest.

The audit had proved damaging
When once it had resumed.
For Murphy clearly cooked the books
As funds he had consumed.

While the funds Murphy diverted
A nest egg to provide.
He'd proven to be arrogant
Where most he did not hide.

Not to mention all the murders
For which he would be tried.
They found the man despicable
In how he killed and lied.

The Mayor screamed profanities
As he was led away.
They would never touch his money
Or he would make them pay.

Matt shook Blake's hand and offered thanks
For all that Blake had done.
The murders may have gone unsolved
For clues they had were none.

THOSE ALSO WHO WERE CULPABLE

He thought he was above it all
And ruled as though a king.
The City Council was a joke
Who'd approve anything.

They were enamored with the perks
That each of them received.
For Murphy had been good to them
So, in him they believed.

He'd hid behind authority
For he's the one in charge.
But no one ever dared to ask
How he'd been living large.

His stipend an embarrassment
To those who'd foot the bill.
For no one ever thought that he
To keep it, stoop to kill.

He was a social predator
Who'd shown he'd no regard
For people he had sworn to serve
He then would disregard.

He claimed the city he restored
To what it once had been.
But the damage that Murphy caused
Had yet to be reeled in.

Where the Council never questioned
A thing Murphy would do.
So, they all had been unaware
Of what he'd been up to.

Blake thought it made them culpable
To all of Murphy's crimes.
Whatever penalty he drew
They should draw equal times.

IN THE AFTERMATH

It had been in the aftermath
Where Gail had thought she'd found
The redemption she'd been seeking
From sins that she'd been bound.

With her love not unrequited
She felt that she had worth.
More than those days of yesteryear
After she'd given birth.

The past had simply been the past
Where she'd no longer dwell.
She had a future facing her
Which promised to be swell.

She had vowed to put behind her
The mistakes that she made.
For she believed her penalties
A thousand times repaid.

Gail thought she'd turned her life around
Now Blake was by her side.
Someone that she could truly love
And in whom could confide.

THE HOAX

Though hoax the legend proved to be,
Exactly as Blake thought.
But people had proved gullible
As into it they bought.

For people are susceptible
When they find they're afraid.
And they'll grasp onto anything
If reason can be made

For even the impossible
Can sometimes panic veer.
As, truly, it's the great unknown
That holds the greatest fear.

For people become terrified
If answers can't be found.
As it is the uncertainty
Around which fear may wound.

The legend, thus, remained alive
Because they had the need.
When something unexplainable
Should once again be keyed.

SOME TIME ALONE

When Blake got home, he found that Gail
Had been waiting for him
He told her ev'rything he knew
Which had seemed pretty grim.

But at least, he said, it's over
With Murphy surely done.
For there could be no argument
Where his freedom was won.

Gail kissed him lightly on his cheek
And said she's proud of him.
With the nightmare truly over
Perhaps it's time for them.

Because so much they had endured
Gail believed they were due.
To spend a little time alone
Where it was just those two.

URBAN LEGEND

After all they had experienced
Some quiet time was due.
The park had seemed the perfect place
For a sweet rendezvous.

The park they thought completely safe
With Murphy locked away.
The man had been a psychopath
Who, somehow, lost his way.

As they walked the park, hand-in-hand,
Blake suddenly had mused
There's something that still bothered him
Which had left him confused.

There was one question that remained
Why did they kill the bear?
For it seemed to serve no purpose
So, why should Murphy dare?

They heard a rustle in the brush
Which caught them by surprise.
Then when they both had turned around
They stared into its eyes.

The thing had been a ghastly beast
That looked reptilian.
Its body was composed of scales
Instead of having skin.

Though its back legs had seemed longer
Than had been the front two.
He saw that as it stood upright
The greater that it grew.

Its snout contained two rows of teeth
With which to rip and tear.
It clearly was a predator
By its unflinching stare.

Its pupils nothing more than slits
In eyes of golden hue.
It showed no sign of compromise
Nor mercy would be due.

It had given them no warning
Before it had appeared.
It caught them by complete surprise
As at them it had sneered.

Blake had thought it urban legend
So, he had failed to act.
When Gail chose to remind him that
Most legends based in fact.

Blake told Gail to step behind him
And then keep very still.
For he'd feared if they saw movement
It'd rally for the kill.

Blake had slowly picked up a limb
That had laid at his feet.
If the creature had been hungry
He'd offer limb to eat.

He stared the creature in the eye
In hope he could disarm.
The fact that it was tracking them
And meant to do them harm.

The creature looked Blake in the eye
But then had looked away.
Perhaps it thought Gail was his mate
And price too great to pay.

Gail looked at Blake as though in shock
And could not mouth a word.
Her hands had shook as though convulsed
And breath had been deferred.

Although the creature was grotesque
It seemed to recognize
There was a danger posed to it
That Blake would not disguise.

All at once they were surrounded
As Blake had counted four.
But in the depth of the darkness
There could be many more.

Gail spun to put her back towards Blake
Prepared for an attack.
But the creatures seemed hesitant
As though taken aback.

Not one of them had made a sound.
They simply stood and stared.
As if they simply studied them
As attack they'd not dared.

The one who stood in front of Blake
Then suddenly would move.
While Blake prepared to swing the limb
As though something to prove.

Then all at once attack was launched
With Blake forced to defend.
He yelled at Gail to stay real close
While with it he'd contend.

Although the creatures slashed at him
And he'd begun to bleed,
It's Gail that he'd fought to protect
As on her they'd not feed.

Their teeth he managed to avoid
But claws like razor wire.
He fought to keep them at arm's length.
Much closer would be dire.

A creature grabbed Gail from behind
While Gail's back had been turned.
She tried her best to fight it off
But freedom had not earned.

The creature had a hold of Gail
As for Blake she cried out.
But he could not get close to her
With creatures all about.

It dragged her towards a sewer drain
Despite how hard she fought.
Until she found her energy
Had been reduced to naught.

It slipped into a sewer grate
That had been pushed aside.
Gail had screamed for him to save her
Then disappeared inside.

A morning patrol had found him
Bleeding and almost dead.
They rushed him to the hospital
While little had he said.

Police had tried to question him
But found it was no use.
It seemed as though he'd lost his mind
So great was his abuse.

Matt and Amy went to see him
Whom he'd not recognized.
As if they were perfect strangers
Or, otherwise, disguised.

When they asked what happened to Gail
His eyes went darkly blank.
That's when Blake began to tremble
And from the pair had shrank.

EPILOG

The man had aged beyond his years
And had appeared infirmed.
They said that he had witnessed it
But that was not confirmed.

His stories were nonsensical
As if he had believed
The urban legends had been real
And they were all deceived.

He would grow worse when came the night
When he would grow disturbed.
Where warnings he would give to them
They dismissed as absurd.

Whatever horrors he had seen
Had caused his mind to fail.
His words incomprehensible
Except for the name Gail.

ABOUT THE AUTHOR

Gordon Bostic was born in West Virginia and grew up in Virginia. A graduate of James Madison University and Fairleigh Dickinson University, he worked as a computer scientist and a software engineer for most of his life. He began writing at a young age as a way of expressing himself, his feelings and his view of the world. Gordon has also had an interest in telling his stories in one way or another. "She Came to Me a Stranger" is his third novel. Gordon currently lives on the Jersey Shore with his wife Susan.